Canine City Survival...
A Holistic Training Manual

by Ken Henry

ISBN 1-59457-018-3

Published by Dog & Daddy Publications, Chicago Illinois

Dog & Daddy

Publications

Contents

FOREWORD

Whether you have a new puppy or an older dog, these canine signs and attached procedures, when practiced in earnest, will help you gain operational control of your pet. Seven commands, taught in the correct order, will assure you of an enhanced relationship and love bond with your pet (family member).

The seven commands are...
1. COME
2. SIT and Lie down
3. STAY
4. HEEL
5. STOP at the curb
6. GOOD BOY / GIRL
7. NO
Commands 6 and 7 are taught in conjunction with "praise" and "reprimand".

With these commands under control you should be able to walk your pet freely with or without a lead and be reasonably assured that they will be safe from the usual dangers that the city has to offer. Your dedication to these necessary steps will naturally enhance your results.

However, anyone who practices these steps will be rewarded with a pet relationship of higher consciousness. Life has no guarantees of results, but even less without the necessary efforts. To those who have adopted an animal/pet-life as a family member "this is for you."

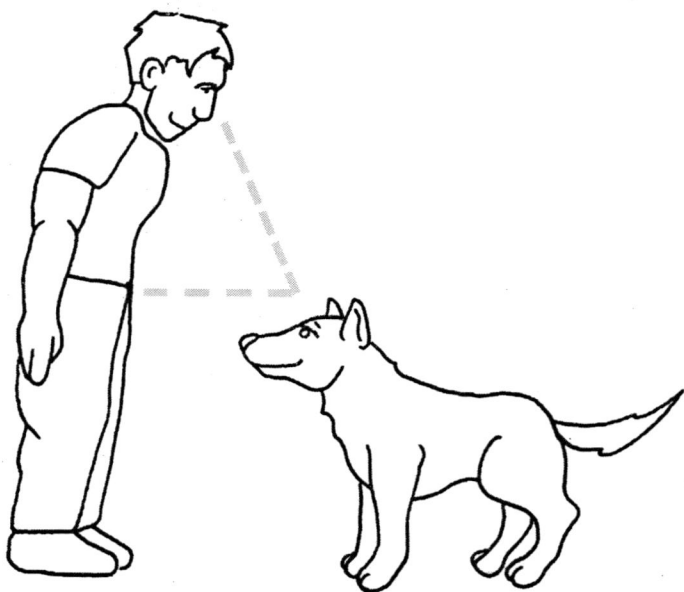

Chapter 1

The Spiritual Triangle

Developing your focus
To send the clearest possible message to your dog it is important to align yourself spiritually on an animal level. I call it the "spiritual triangle". In martial arts it is referred to as the "Trinity Triangle"—That is to deliver the signals with your mind-gut, and heart simultaneously.

In a diagram, it would appear to be a three-fold triangle leading from your lower stomach, your forehead, and your heart converging in an apex at the mind of your dog. Your dog can hear your heart beat from about 15 feet away so projecting "spiritually" is very important.

Speaking to your dog
It is important to aim your triangle by bending down toward your dog as you speak. The motion of the source of sound is called the "doppler effect", which dogs do every time they bark. Although dogs can hear far better than we can, they respond much better to "directed-doppler" sound. When delivering commands to your dog from a distance,

cup your hands like a megaphone, again aiming your triangle.

To help you achieve the correct mindset and emphasize how to use the "spiritual triangle" properly, place your fingertips about an inch below your navel and press to gain focus. When giving a command never allow your voice to trail upward in pitch. Your dog should hear strength, dominance and resolution, and you should feel it. The stronger you are, the more your dog will trust and believe in you. At this point your dog is not able to be your best friend but rather a new recruit in your platoon. You are the Sergeant and they must listen to you. However, unlike a Sergeant, you will be *using happy but firm energy* whenever possible.

Practicing this procedure will help you find that fine line between animal gut-reaction and personal self-control. It is a way of projecting the strength of your mind to your animal. Working in this way when taken to its greatest degree can give you an almost psychic mode of operation as your dog literally learns to anticipate your next desire for him.

Animals are very sensitive to this spiritual connection as their spirits are much more directly connected universally than most human beings are. This is a relationship which I have enjoyed with my own dogs (best friends).

Chapter 2
Love Bond Development

Becoming the animal
Learning about and using canine body language is a
prerequisite in training at both developmental and higher
levels. Carefully examining our own animal responses or
observing mothers with litters or older dogs with younger
dogs will give you a guideline on how dogs think and work.

These "observed" tools coupled with carefully delivered
"human logic" will very specifically convey your message of
love and pack bonding. These steps of both "praise" and
"reprimand" should become a natural response to you in
communication with your animal.

Establishing a head of the pack mentality
There are many words used like "alpha" or "pack-leader"
or whatever, but what they all mean is YOU are in charge. In

the beginning of your training program it is important to press the issue of "canine parenthood".

Your canine body language with your animal should include:
- Placing your head over the animals head
- Face contact - with the dogs ears, top of the dogs head, back of the dogs neck and over the dogs eyes.

Many of you probably already practice these canine body languages as you interact with your pet. Going forward, knowing what these signs mean, as you continue to practice them your dog will feel and smell your confidence and respond appropriately. This is of course much easier with younger dogs or puppies.

Whenever giving a vocal command, especially when in the developmental stages of training you should bend down over your dog (spiritual triangle) so they feel your presence near their head and your general close encroachment. I also use a hand or body signal (non verbal) to reinforce my commands. Over time I separate the verbal/signal commands so my dog will respond to either independently.

If there is any question of a dog's emotional stability or hostility, appropriate cautionary measures should be practiced. Hold the dogs muzzle (nose and lower jaw) closed, while grasping the collar tightly, "before and after" head contact should definitely be practiced on dogs with any kind of questionable behavioral traits. I would only recommend muzzling as a last resort.

Soothing techniques

Soothing techniques, such as *Grounding your dog* by laying over the dog with your head over the dogs or rolling the dog over on their back, also helps to create the pecking order or instinctive "leader of pack mentality". The goal is to dominate with love.

These soothing techniques work especially well in cases of insubordinate or unfocused behavior and are explained in detail in Chapter 5: How to Reprimand.

Tips to support your own dominant response:
- Deposit some saliva on the fur of the dog's head
  (I do so by licking my hand and rubbing my dog's head)
- Hooking your hand over the back of their neck.
- Giving commands and reprimands by leaning over
  their head.

Dogs use these procedures to establish dominance developing a pecking order as it were, to help secure an operative relationship between you and your dog.

It is also a good idea to give your dog regular physical examinations to get him/her used to being examined as well as to keep you informed of any manifestations like lumps or sore spots that may be forming. This can be done most easily by petting your dog and checking them at the same time.

Chapter 3

Praise Mode
Encouragement

Praise
All these techniques should be delivered with "loving enthusiasm" and "strongly expressed words of praise". They should become as automatic as breathing. Praise should be unrestrained and training sessions should be as much like playing as possible. Also praise your dog for no particular reason as they live for praise and just hearing it makes your dog happier. Both your attitude and focus is what your dog depends on.

Training Sessions using Praise Mode
Try to very carefully gauge your dog's attention span. For young dogs or puppies, training sessions should be short; *perhaps 5-10 minutes twice a day. Individual dogs vary in this respect, so try to be sensitive to this. Puppies actual specific memory is about 20–30 seconds; so long term punishments are neither beneficial nor applicable and can be detrimental over time.

If your dog gets frustrated or appears to be confused or overloaded, it is wise to give the dog an intermission. Then enthusiastically praise the dog so they know that even just "trying to perform" they are doing the right thing and therefore pleasing you.

To correctly end a session you should stop your dog's activities and then give the dog something simple to do like sit or whatever you prefer. Once accomplished, then triple over praise your dog with happy energy and then dismiss the class and let him/her play or whatever. I'd usually tell my dog, Reef to "Go be a dog". Always end on a good note…

Never reward your animal for getting things wrong. Always make sure to practice specific consistency when not in session. Your dog should earn their way off lead and whenever given a command, execute it properly.

Rewards

You might notice that I don't mention food rewards. I consider them a very last resort especially when training a puppy. The reason is, in order to create a love-operational bond, food can be used, but only early on as a maternal bonding process and not on a constant basis.

Food = instinct / prey drive
Toys = intellect / fun

The best reward is to use an abundance of love or the dogs favorite toy. Toys will expand their intellect. Importantly, using a toy makes your dog less likely to be taken off focus by food smells. And less tamper-able by strangers, who may have food to tempt your dog, but are not likely to have their favorite toy with them to get your dogs attention.

If a dog is "audio responsive" I'll employee a squeaky toy to initially teach focus. This is a good way to get the dogs attention when they become distracted. However, only squeak the toy in single squeaks or intermittently not constantly, so they don't become tired of the tone. Once the dog is drawn by the sound, continue into the activity you want them to perform with happy, strong energy.

Your dog should never interact with strangers without your direct permission, especially while they are young or in training. If a stranger calls to your dog, politely explain to them that your dog is in behavior modification training. If they are put off by your response, simply ignore these people completely. They are not the ones who will be living with this animal, you are.

Giving your dog a treat once in a while is fine, but not as a direct reward for a command or a trick. My dog worked for "Frisbees". We all work for something...

YOUR FOCUS IS THEIR FOCUS...

Chapter 4

Discipline
Without without breaking their Spirit

No dog learns perfectly. As your dog shows disobedience, you must establish a parental type authority as quickly as possible. This of course is easier with a puppy than an older dog. I don't recommend anyone taking on a pet/life, without getting at least a rudimentary education on their animals behavior and instincts.

For example, to drive a car we have to take a test, cars don't breathe, eat, sleep or keep you company, or even love you. Your dog deserves the best from you, and of course so do you from them. You must make the effort to learn animal language and instincts in order to teach it.

Reprimand (Punishment / Guidance)
Just as you establish focus by physically placing your head over your dogs neck, ears, head, etc., reprimand is very similar with a few exceptions.

When an infraction or crime, has been committed it is naturally better to catch the dog in the act. However, if you were to find a chewed shoe, piece of furniture, or some other object which they have obviously had unauthorized mouth contact, the dogs own scent of saliva and body pheromone will be present and will warrant reprimand as the crime is still obviously clear. Keep in mind that your dog has over one million times the ability to smell than you.* Your dog will know what they did. If you have more than one dog, punish them all. Canines respond to peer pressure.

Preparing to Reprimand
DO NOT call your dog to punish them, walk over to them. Control your emotional nature by taking two deep breaths or by counting to five. This is very important because your dog is constantly reading your smell (pheromones), their favorite smell is when you are upset, angry, or agitated. This smell is very pleasant to your dog.* Your dog may even do bad things to provoke this scent. The dog's reaction is similar to a child working for bad attention.

By breathing or counting, you change your emotional nature and therefore your pheromone/smell changes too. The reprimand is much more controlled, military style, rather than personal. This controlled emotional state makes you much more dependable and believable to your dog.

Chapter 5
How to Reprimand

The EAR BITE technique
The ear bite technique is
used for high-level offenses,
like endangering themselves or others, or deliberate
disobedience. The ear bite technique is far less offensive and
much more understandable to your dog's instincts than,
shock collars, spike or prong collars, hanging or neck—
swinging, hitting, kicking, long term confinement, or any
number of abominations that are practiced every day by the
military, the police, as well as private trainers.

The properly delivered "ear-bite"
1) First, attach the lead to your dog.
2) Hold the snout (nose and lower jaw) firmly closed, draw
   your dog's ears to your mouth. With your other hand
   grasping the collar.
3) Say "NO" sharply then bite the ear with "purpose" but
   not cruelty.

The strength of the bite will vary, depending on the offense. Most dogs or puppies will not require this level of stimuli, but it is good to have this in your training toolbox.

Life and limb threatening situations naturally require a harder bite. It is possible, but probably not as effective, to substitute a pinch, but your head proximity is very important, as feeling your breath on their ears and sensing your close presence is essential when delivering this reprimand. Never break the dog's skin or draw blood. Merely use the ear bite technique to provoke a mild whine or yelp.

This is a teaching tool, it is wise to use this reprimand with restraint, because it is for serious breeches of conduct like jumping on or knocking down children, and or serious aggressive behavior, and not minor corrections. Once they understand the nature of this reprimand it may only become necessary to lean toward your dog and reach for their ear and they will respond positively.

Naturally you will be using this more while they are in the developmental stages of their training. In my experience I've found that it is best not to give a "reprimand" if the situation does not allow you to do so correctly.

Aggressive behavior between dogs (to be corrected):
-Dogs head over neck or back of another dog
-Dogs foot on the back of another dog, (prelude to mounting)
-Mounting another dog
-Chest pushing from front or side and subsequent shoving
-Direct charging without stopping to sniff (prey drive)
-Flank crowding, steering or herding from behind
-Raised hackles, hair on neck or back
-Stiff legged walking with fixed stare
-Growling during any of these activities
-Bedeviling—Running next to, barking aggressively and jumping on
  from the side interfering with legs in motion

Techniques for Lesser Offenses:

The "Scruff Shake"
For lesser offenses use the "scruff shake" method. Grasp the collar of your dog and give them a sharp vocal reprimand with your head directly over the dogs head and with your breath on their ears, shake moderately while saying the word "no". Mother's often shake their pups in just this way, so it is again, part of their nature and easily understand.

Grounding your dog
If your dog doesn't appear cooperative or seems to still be somehow distracted, the logical next step is "grounding" him, which is practiced by females when controlling pups. Maintaining the hold on your dog's collar, sweep the dog to the ground and lay over the them with their ear against your mouth while you immobilize the dog's body with yours, and try to maintain this position till the dog is motionless. Speaking softly and slowly during this procedure helps.

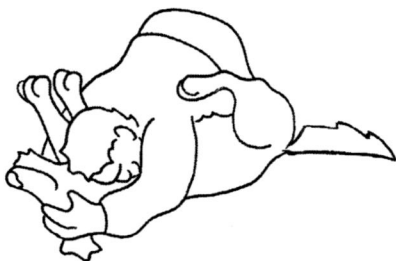

A mild, "ear bite" may help, but since this a soothing technique, you can try humming in the dogs ear and stroking them slowing while you "ground" the dog. As mentioned before, this grounding technique works well in cases of deliberate disobedience, as well as unfocused behavior. I've found that in most cases that soothing, then re-establishing your training session works best.

Naturally, it is important to use the *appropriate cautionary measures* when practicing any disciplinary instruction. Every dog is different and every owner's bond is unique, but all these practices have an accumulative effect in shaping the cooperative relationship between you and your pet.

These very disciplines are practiced every day by female dogs with their litters and go back five-million years in canine instincts. This would include praise as well as reprimands. Again reinforcing the philosophy that you need to learn animal language in order to teach one.

As time goes on and your dog becomes more malleable to command, you may only need to distract them from negative behavior by a vocal reprimand, shaking your keys, squeezing the squeaky toy, or throwing an empty can with a few pennies inside, in their near vicinity as a reminder. This would fall into the category of "subtle back", as discussed in the last chapter.

Although I only cover the basic seven commands in this book, these character shaping concepts apply directly to higher levels of training as well. They are a blueprint to your operational relationship both initially as well as ongoing. Also remember to be innovative in your pursuit of common sense ways of teaching. Keeping an open mind will help expand your relationship as well as keep your dog interested.

They'll love you for it...

Chapter 6

Biting

The "bite example"

A handy method in the case of biting, particularly in younger dogs or puppies is the "bite example". First, adopt the previously mentioned body language taught for "reprimand". Then place the dog's paw in his/her mouth. Squeeze down on the dog's nose and jaw forcing the dog to bite their paw hard enough to provoke a whine or yelp. Breaking the skin is not at all necessary.

Using a spray bottle

For larger and more difficult to handle dogs I recommend using a spray bottle with a mixture of vinegar and pepper, (one quart white vinegar/one tablespoon pepper, and some hot sauce) — which also works well as a salad dressing <yummy>.

Set the bottle nozzle on jet as opposed to mist and give the dog a good shot in the face, primarily the nose. This also works well as a general "distance" reprimand if your dog acts in an evasive manner. You might want to carry this bottle with you or have several bottles placed at key easy access positions in your home till your dog passes the phase of needing this stimuli.

It will probably get to the point that you only have to reach for the bottle to get a positive response. Since these are food substances rather than chemicals like *mace* or *scat*, they have no toxic effects.

Since canines are regularly "skunked", in the wild they will easily understand this. Depending on the dog the pepper can be, **Black – mild intensity, Cayenne – medium intensity or Habaneras – strong intensity.**

Experience helps and the whole family should be well versed in these previously mentioned techniques, making sure that everyone practices the same method with consistency. If it's not worth the effort, in my opinion **"don't have a dog!"**

Chapter 7
Toilet Training, ooops...

Going to the bathroom in your home is just your dog's way of establishing their territory. You must re-establish your territory as soon as possible. To start you will need the white vinegar again and your focus.

When you find the "crime", walk over to your dog quietly. Then place the lead on your dog and take them to the "scene". Put the dogs nose near it, but not in it as I feel that is cruel and only necessary in extremely drastic cases. Holding the dog there, clean up the mess. Then soak the "crime scene", well with vinegar.

Place the dogs nose close to the puddle of vinegar and say "NO" very sharply, with your face directly over the dog's ears. *Since this is a discipline tactic appropriate cautions should be practiced.* After which give them a good solid "scruff shake" and a mild "toss away". Immediately throw the mess outside, or wherever you want your dog to go. Ignore your dog for about 15 seconds. Then give him/her a simple task like "sit".

After your dog responds to the simple task, enthusiastically praise them with all the love you have, using all the love domination signs.

"Season well" with vinegar every place in your home where your dog has gone or is likely to go—to give them a "smell" reminder. *

Following these steps consistently will eventually get your dog toilet trained.

I said "focus"!

Chapter 8

Preparing to Train

When beginning a training session prepare yourself appropriately. Wear comfortable clothing that you don't mind getting dirty, with places to carry things and solid footwear that gives you control—no flip flops. Your hands should be free of any objects like cell phones, sunglasses, jewelry, or whatever you might carry.

If the lead pulling you or whatever activity you're involved in with your dog causes hand discomfort, wear gloves. I recommend these procedures whenever training your dog or even just walking them.

Equipment:
1 leather collar (no tags)
One round (like a rope) **leather collar** that fits close but not

too snug. Your dog has over ten times the ability to hear and can hear sound spectrums far higher and lower than you, tags should be immobilized for quiet operation.

1 ten-foot lead (not retractable)
1 thirty-foot lead (not retractable)

or as last resort
1 nylon choke collar
(Round like a rope, not flat like a strap)

Chapter 9

Come

Oooh...
Here
he comes

The "COME" command is relatively simple.

Attach a thirty-foot lead to your dog, and let it stray out till the lead is fully extended. Then call your dog's name and say "COME" (or whatever word you prefer to use).

If your dog does not respond, as much as you would like to DO NO REPEAT the command. Simply, reel the dog in with the lead. As your dog approaches, encourage their progress by slapping your legs and saying loving words like "here you come" or whatever comes easiest for you, using very loving tones making sure that you don't repeat the actual come command.

When your dog arrives at your side, go immediately and enthusiastically into the previously stated "praise mode". This command should always be taught on lead, and without "reprimand". Practice this command in an enclosed area and make your dog earn their way off his/her lead. DO NOT; try to walk your dog off lead, till this command is under control.

If your dog becomes distracted the "penny can" distraction works well in this situation. However if the penny can becomes a "plaything", discontinue its use in this application. A squeaky toy may work well in this situation. However, don't throw the toy to your dog. Just use the sound as an incentive.

Also you can take a long lead and attach a set of keys.* Throw the keys in your dog's direction and drag the lead back toward you while saying encouraging things to your dog. The dog will usually follow the jingling keys back to you. You can also use a toy that squeaks in this capacity. Remember to praise your dog. The lead is necessary, at least initially, to guide the dog to proper execution.

If your dog is off lead and is resisting the command, you may try encouraging words, while running away from your dog. Move your feet in a capering motion or shuffling them, as well as maybe drag your keys or squeak a toy while running away. Since most dogs love moving objects as well as chasing, this usually helps to motivate them. You can also try sitting or lying on the ground to encourage your pet to come and investigate you. Experiment...

Chapter 10

Sit

Sit is an easy command to teach...

Start with your dog on a lead. Maneuver your dog close to you and then grasp the collar with your hand and say the word "SIT" with authority in your voice, again dopplering down. At the same time, slide your free hand down your dogs back as you kneel down, causing the dog to sit. When the dog is sitting, you should be kneeling next to the dog with your head over their head, facing the dog from the side.

The collar grasp, hand slide, and kneeling should all be done in one single motion. Once completed you should go immediately into the "praise mode" with full enthusiasm. If your dog is uncooperative, go directly into "reprimand" or if the dog is hyperactive, but not aggressive, then perhaps a soothing out technique can be adopted. As all dogs are different, try to be sensitive to this to see what works best.

All these procedures should be practiced in a very "matter of fact" non-hesitating kind of way. The amount of repetitions to accomplish this will vary, depending on the temperament of the dog and the procedural enthusiasm of the owner.

"For your dog to be fully involved;
You must be fully involved."

Chapter 11
Lie
Down

I'm including this command even though I don't consider it to be one of the primary seven.

The lie down command is most easily taught from the "canine" sit position. Simply reach under your dog while holding their collar, sweep their front legs forward and say "LIE DOWN" with authority in your voice. If your dog shows reluctance, I suggest lying down over your dog as you sweep their legs forward while say loving encouraging words during the execution. Soothing out procedures work very well in this sequence.

Chapter 12

Stay

Sit and stay, are usually companion commands and stay is ordinarily accomplished from the canine "sit" position...

Once you have accomplished "SIT" and have praised your dog, place your hand toward the dogs face and say the word "STAY", with purpose in your voice. Then, back slowly away from the dog, trailing the lead behind you. As you back away lower your head so your eyes are more level with the dogs, maintaining your hand in the stay command position. If your dog does not stay, walk back to the dog, mildly "reprimand" them, and then manually replace the dog into their previous "stay" position and repeat the process.

Sometimes placing your hand directly over the dogs eyes works well on stubborn or hearing-impaired dogs. If your dog tends to jump or struggle out of stay, soothing out techniques may also be employed. Humming with the dogs ear in your mouth is another excellent soothing method which applies well in this situation. Praise and affection should always be conscientiously exercised.

Employing a second party to hold your dog from behind can be very helpful. However, it is important that anyone participating in your dog's education be well aware of all the steps of "praise" and "reprimand". This is especially necessary for family dogs or members of multiple house-holds. Again, make these steps second nature and repeat them with specific consistency and never forget to count or breathe before reprimand.

GOOD LUCK.

Chapter 13
Heel

In my opinion the command "heel" is merely an extension of "stay", only it's "stay, with you". With my own canine relationships, I personally use the command "stay with me" or "come with me".

Teaching heel
One method is to hold the lead on the opposite side of your body in one hand, and bring it around behind your hips, to your other hand. You can use both hands in a swiveling motion to control the dogs position. When employing this method you can also hold the lead from the opposite side and as your dog pulls forward you can hold your hand (I would employ a baseball cap) directly in front of the dog's face interrupting their line of sight to greater control their point of reference as far as positioning is concerned. The cap works doubly well as it not only obscures their sight but also smells like your head. Since your dog will be pulling the lead through your body at a point where your center of gravity is lower, you will have a greater physical advantage. You can also turn toward the dog and the lead will wind around you in a "winching" effect, reeling the dog in while still having

the mechanical advantage. You will end up facing your dog blocking their view of what they are being drawn toward. You could then kneel down in front of your dog, making eye contact and further controlling them.

Another method would be, holding the loop, then wrap the lead around your upper arm, close to your armpit, then back to your hand. Then hold the lead on the same side as your dog, but pulling with your shoulder, giving you greater leverage.

Start with your dog at the side of your own choosing, with their head even with your leg in a position that they can easily see your hand from. Then say "HEEL", or whatever word you choose, and proceed to walk. If your dog pulls you, STOP abruptly and say "NO" sharply. Then a short "reprimand". You can also use a squeaky toy to draw the dogs attention back to you and then give the dog instruction in a happy way to continue the progress.

If your dog hangs back, try shuffling your feet as you happily say encouraging words or again squeak the toy. Then repeat the command and continue. A series of repetitions should help the progress. *A method of encouragement with which I have had great success is to press my dog's head against the outside of my thigh as we walk, petting his head and verbally encouraging him to walk with me, initially to be done in conjunction with the lead for guidance.* Naturally it is difficult to impossible to do this with a small dog, but the mindset, praise, and encouragement factors always apply.

A last resort method is to blindfold your dog while using these steps. Remember to "breathe or count", to keep yourself stabilized and don't forget to praise heavily. Be patient. The rewards will come.

Chapter 14

Stop/Stop at the Curb

This command is a combination of "HEEL" and "STAY"
First, attach the lead to your dog. Next walk briskly toward
the curb. Upon arrival at the curb, "STOP" abruptly. If your
dog passes the curb say "NO" sharply, almost barking the
word and, at the same moment tug the lead again with
purpose, not cruelty. Then bring your dog back to the curb,
physically replacing them in the original STOP, SIT, and STAY
position. Make the dog "SIT"and "STAY". Using happy
strong energy can make it fun for them to stop.

Trailing the lead behind you, cross the curb, backing away
from your dog, till the lead is fully extended. As you back
away again as in "stay", lower your eye contact to corre-
spond more with your dog's height, with your hand in the
stay command position. Then wait an appropriate amount
of time (usually about 10 seconds, after which, call your dog

to you making it absolutely clear that your dog can only cross the curb with your permission.

In the case of my own dog I use the word "CLEAR" whenever he is slated to cross a curb or an obstacle so as to create a separate command. If someone should attempt to call your dog across a street this tends to act as a safeguard.

As your dog becomes more accustomed to this command you should vary the time interval of the stay, so the dog does not anticipate your permission and enter the street prematurely, as the motion of cars and people can be an attractive distraction. All the usual stay procedures apply of course.

Repeat these steps until you can run at the curb and stop; and your dog will stop with you. Naturally, all "praise" and "reprimand" procedures apply.

Chapter 15

Subtle Back
Increasing Command Awareness

Initially, when teaching a command, clear and forceful delivery of your message should be practiced. However, as time passes and your dog(s) awareness of your commands increase, begin to use less and less force to get your points across. Carefully monitor their responses, till it takes very little effort to get your dog's attention and keep it.

Speaking to your dog conversationally is a good way to bring up the dogs perceptions. The dog will learn to pick up on key words as well as understand the words context and your delivery. I've always talked to my canine friends, as they are the best listeners— they tend not to interrupt, and they are excellent when it comes to taking suggestion. Begin to practice this only when they are already strong in their obedience to command.

Being more and more subtle helps to bring up your dogs attention span as well as their comprehension. It is this method that will truly bring out the dogs intellect. It may eventually become procedure for you to merely whisper commands or make very slight hand or eye motions to get your point across.
Practice this in earnest!

EPILOGUE

I've listed these commands in a specific order, so your dog will become more and more operationally obedient as the command difficulty increases. Please do not teach these commands out of this order. You were unable to run or drive, before you could crawl or walk. Your dog should "come", "sit" and "stay" before "heeling", or "stopping at the curb".

- Remember to "praise" and "reprimand" both vocally and physically during the training process in an "automatic" response kind of way.

- Remember to "breathe" or "count" when upset or agitated; and to over-enthusiastically praise with unbridled spirit.

- Remember to praise your dog for no particular reason.

- Remember the amount of focus and automatic response you put out will invariably be reflected in your dog's performance, as your dog is a direct reflection of your effort and dedication.

- Most importantly—Remember to love your dog, but also be their parent; as your dog is in every way your "child". Your pet's life is a "gift" that is in your "hands".

Again, Good Luck...
   Ken Henry
   Reef-1, Lady Barquelotte, Coral Reef I "Fluffy", Coral Reef II "Also Fluffy" and Coral Reef III "Rock Dog"

Sources of information

* Paul Loeb's Complete Book of Dog Training

Various mother and father dogs.

My own observations, experiments and personal experiences.

'Martial art's instructor Al Mcluckie .

And last but not least...
God's gift of four fantastic canine friends...

1021005

Made in the USA